A poet in his own right, RICHMOND LATTIMORE *is Paul Shorey Professor of Greek at Bryn Mawr College, and co-editor and translator of many of the plays in* The Complete Greek Tragedies *now being published in series by The University of Chicago Press. His translations of* The Iliad *and* The Odes of Pindar *as well as of the Greek drama have received high critical praise.*

GREEK LYRICS

GREEK LYRICS

Translated
into close approximations of
the original meter

By Alexander
Richmond Lattimore

THE UNIVERSITY OF CHICAGO PRESS

Library of Congress Catalog Number: 55-11465

THE UNIVERSITY OF CHICAGO PRESS, CHICAGO 37
Cambridge University Press, London, N.W. 1, England
The University of Toronto Press, Toronto 5, Canada

PREFACE

For about a century and a half, roughly from the middle of the seventh century B.C. to the end of the sixth, the dominant form of literature in Greece was the independent short poem. We may call them "lyrics," though to the Greeks themselves this term would have described only those poems which were meant to be sung or chanted to the accompaniment of a lyre. Before this period, or so I think, came the age of epic, culminating in the two great Homeric poems; after it came the perfection of drama and the development of prose, for science, speculation, historical narrative, and persuasion. The lyrics of our period were of the most varied kind. We may find them secular or sacred; provincial or cosmopolitan; personal or objectively public; mere sequences of lines or couplets or elaborate stanzas or strophes; and in various dialects. Yet in a way they have a kind of unity, because of the period in which they belong, because of their relative brevity and self-sufficiency, and because of the shared accident of their destruction. We have manuscripts proper only for Theognis and Pindar, and for Pindar all but the victory odes are fragmentary. For other poets, we have only a collection of quotations from subsequent authors and scraps of papyrus from Alexandrian Egypt—mostly fragments, but sometimes poems quoted or preserved in full. The following ninety-one lyrics are offered here in translation in the hope that they may give some notion of what this poetry was like.

Some of these translations have appeared previously in the *Hudson Review* and the *Quarterly Review of Literature*.

TABLE OF CONTENTS

ARCHILOCHUS

EPIGRAMS

· 1 ·

I am two things: a fighter who follows the Master of Battles,
and one who understands the gift of the Muses' love.

· 2 ·

By spear is kneaded the bread I eat, by spear my Ismaric
wine is won, which I drink, leaning upon my spear.

· 3 ·

Some barbarian is waving my shield, since I was obliged to
leave that perfectly good piece of equipment behind
under a bush. But I got away, so what does it matter?
Let the shield go; I can buy another one equally good.

4 · *On a Willing Woman*

Wild fig tree of the rocks, so often feeder of ravens,
Loves-them-all, the seducible, the stranger's delight.

5 · *Epitaph*

O vast earth, you contain Arístophon and Megatímos
under your folds, the two tall columns of Naxos sustained.

6 · *Charon the Smith*

Nothing to me the life of Gyges and his glut
of gold. I neither envy nor admire him, as
I watch his life and what he does. I want no pride
of tyranny; it lies far off from where I look.

7 · *Two Captains*

I don't like the towering captain with the spraddly length of leg,
one who swaggers in his lovelocks and cleanshaves beneath the chin.
Give me a man short and squarely set upon his legs, a man
full of heart, not to be shaken from the place he plants his feet.

POEMS

8 · *On Friends Lost at Sea*

Blaming the bitterness of this sorrow, Perikles, no man
   in all our city can take pleasure in festivities:
Such were the men the surf of the roaring sea washed under,
   all of us go with hearts aching against our ribs
for misery. Yet against such grief that is past recovery
   the gods, dear friend, have given us strong endurance to be
our medicine. Such sorrows are variable. They beat now
   against ourselves, and we take the hurt of the bleeding sore.
Tomorrow it will be others who grieve, not we. From now on
   act like a man, and put away these feminine tears.

· 9 ·

Heart, my heart, so battered with misfortune far beyond your strength,
up, and face the men who hate us. Bare your chest to the assault
of the enemy, and fight them off. Stand fast among the beamlike spears.
Give no ground; and if you beat them, do not brag in open show,
nor, if they beat you, run home and lie down on your bed and cry.
Keep some measure in the joy you take in luck, and the degree
you give way to sorrow. All our life is up-and-down like this.

10 · *Eclipse of the Sun*

Nothing will surprise me any more, nor be too wonderful
for belief, now that the lord upon Olympus, father Zeus,
dimmed the daylight and made darkness come upon us in the noon
and the sunshine. So limp terror has descended on mankind.
After this, men can believe in anything. They can expect
anything. Be not astonished any more, although you see

beasts of the dry land exchange with dolphins, and assume their place in the watery pastures of the sea, and beasts who loved the hills find the ocean's crashing waters sweeter than the bulk of land.

FRAGMENTS

· 11 ·

I will make nothing better by crying, I will make nothing
worse by giving myself what entertainment I can.

· 12 ·

Often along the streaming hair of the gray salt water
they pray for sweet homecoming won in spite of the sea.

· 13 ·

Glaukos, a soldier of fortune's your friend as long as he's fighting.

14 · *Thasos*

Here the island stands
stiff with wild timber like a donkey's bristling back.
This is no place of beauty, not desirable
nor lovely like the plains where the River Siris runs.

· 15 ·

Glaukos, look! The open sea is churning to a wash of waves
deep within. A cloud stands upright over the Gyrean cape,
signal of a storm, and terror rises from the unforeseen.

· 16 ·

Luxurious in a spray of myrtle, she wore too
the glory of the rose upon her, and her hair
was all a darkness on her shoulders and her back.

· 17 ·

The fox knows many tricks, the hedgehog only one.
One good one.

· 18 ·

Say goodbye to Paros, and the figs, and the seafaring life.

19 · *Thasos*

All the griefs of all the Hellenes came together in this place.

20 · *Thasos*

Let not the stone of Tantalos
overhang this island any longer.

· 21 ·

We, a thousand, are the murderers of the seven men who fell
dead. We overtook them with our running feet. . . .

22 · *On Drowned Bodies*

Hide we away these painful gifts of the lord Poseidon.

23 · *The Wreckers and a Former Friend*

. . .

slammed by the surf on the beach
naked at Salmydéssos, where the screw-haired men
of Thrace, taking him in
will entertain him (he will have much to undergo,
chewing on slavery's bread)
stiffened with cold, and loops of seaweed from the slime
tangling his body about,
teeth chattering as he lies in abject helplessness
flat on his face like a dog
beside the beach-break where the waves come shattering in.
And let me be there to watch;
for he did me wrong and set his heel on our good faith,
he who had once been my friend.

· 24 ·

Here I lie mournful with desire,
feeble in bitterness of the pain gods inflicted upon me,
stuck through the bones with love.

· 25 ·

If it only were my fortune just to touch Neoboule's hand.

· 26 ·

Such is the passion for love that has twisted its way beneath
    my heartstrings
and closed deep mist across my eyes
stealing the soft heart from inside my body. . . .

· 27 ·

My lord Apollo, single out the guilty ones;
destroy them, O destroyer god.

28 · *The Fox Appeals for Justice*

O Zeus, our father Zeus, for you control the sky,
you oversee the works of men,
    the right acts and the wrong they do; so yours to judge
the crimes and punishment of beasts.

· 29 ·

Father Lykámbes, whatever were you thinking of?
And who seduced the common sense
in which you once were so secure? How things are changed!
Your neighbors giggle in your face.

· 30 ·

To the gods all things are easy. Many times from circumstance
of disaster they set upright those who have been sprawled at length
on the ground, but often again when men stand planted on firm feet,
these same gods will knock them on their backs, and then the
    evils come,
so that a man wanders homeless, destitute, at his wit's end.

· 31 ·

Érxias, where is all this useless army gathering to go?

· 32 ·

No man is respected, no man spoken of, when he is dead
by his townsmen. All of us, when still alive, will cultivate
the live man, and thus the dead will always have the worst of it.

· 33 ·

One main thing I understand,
to come back with deadly evil at the man who does me wrong.

CALLINUS

How long will you lie idle, and when will you find some courage,
   you young men? Have you no shame of what other cities will say,
you who hang back? You think you can sit quiet in peacetime.
   This is not peace, it is war which has engulfed our land.

A man, as he dies, should make one last throw with his spear.
It is a high thing, a bright honor, for a man to do battle
   with the enemy for the sake of his children, and for his land
and his true wife; and death is a thing that will come when the spinning
   Destinies make it come. So a man should go straight on
forward, spear held high, and under his shield the fighting
   strength coiled ready to strike in the first shock of the charge.
When it is ordained that a man shall die, there is no escaping
   death, not even for one descended from deathless gods.
Often a man who has fled from the fight and the clash of the thrown
      spears
goes his way, and death befalls him in his own house,
and such a man is not loved nor missed for long by his people;
   the great and the small alike mourn when a hero dies.
For all the populace is grieved for the high-hearted warrior
   after his death; while he lives, he is treated as almost divine.
Their eyes gaze on him as if he stood like a bastion before them.
   His actions are like an army's, though he is only one man.

SEMONIDES OF AMORGOS

1 · *An Essay on Women*

In the beginning God made various kinds of women
with various minds. He made one from the hairy sow,
that one whose house is smeared with mud, and all within
lies in dishevelment and rolls along the ground,
while the pig-woman in unlaundered clothing sits
unwashed herself among the dunghills, and grows fat.

God made another woman from the mischievous
vixen, whose mind gets into everything. No act
of wickedness unknown to her; no act of good
either, because the things she says are often bad
but sometimes good. Her temper changes all the time.

One from a bitch, and good-for-nothing like her mother.
She must be in on everything, and hear it all.
Out she goes ranging, poking her nose everywhere
and barking, whether she sees anyone about
or not. Her husband cannot make her stop by threats,
neither when in a rage he knocks her teeth out with
a stone, nor when he reasons with her in soft words,
not even when there's company come, and she's with
     them.
Day in, day out, she keeps that senseless yapping up.

The gods of Olympus made another one of mud
and gave her lame to man. A woman such as this
knows nothing good and nothing bad. Nothing at all.
The only thing she understands is how to eat,
and even if God makes the weather bad, she won't,
though shivering, pull her chair up closer to the fire.

One from the sea. She has two different sorts of mood.
One day she is all smiles and happiness. A man
who comes to visit sees her in the house and says:
"There is no better wife than this one anywhere
in all mankind, nor prettier." Then, another day

there'll be no living with her, you can't get within
sight, or come near her, or she flies into a rage
and holds you at a distance like a bitch with pups,
cantankerous and cross with all the world. It makes
no difference whether they are friends or enemies.
The sea is like that also. Often it lies calm
and innocent and still, the mariner's delight
in summer weather. Then again it will go wild
and turbulent with the thunder of big crashing waves.
This woman's disposition is just like the sea's,
since the sea's temper also changes all the time.

One was a donkey, dusty-gray and obstinate.
It's hard to make her work. You have to curse and tug
to make her do it, but in the end she gets it done
quite well. Then she goes to her corner-crib and eats.
She eats all day, she eats all night, and by the fire
she eats. But when there's a chance to make love, she'll
        take
the first one of her husband's friends who comes along.

One from a weasel—miserable, stinking thing.
There's nothing pretty about her. She has no kind
of charm, no kind of sweetness, and no sex appeal.
She's always crazy to make love and go to bed,
but makes her husband—if she has one—sick, when he
comes near her. And she steals from neighbors. She's
        all bad.
She robs the altar and eats up the sacrifice.

One was begotten from the maned, fastidious mare.
She manages to avoid all housework and the chores
of slaves. She wouldn't touch the mill, or lift a sieve,
or sweep the dung from the house and throw it out of doors,
or kneel by the fire. Afraid the soot will make her dirty.
She makes her husband boon-companion to Hard Times.
She washes the dirt off her body every day
twice at least, three times some days, and anoints herself
with perfume, and forever wears her long hair combed
and shadowed deep with flowers. A woman such as this
makes, to be sure, a lovely wife for someone else

to look at, but her husband finds her an expense
unless he is some baron or a sceptered king
who can indulge his taste for luxuries like her.

One was a monkey; and this is the very worst,
most exquisite disaster Zeus has wished on men.
Hers is the ugliest face of all. When such a woman
walks through the village, everybody turns to laugh.
Her neck's so short that she can scarcely turn her head.
Slab-sided, skinny-legged. Oh, unhappy man
who has to take such a disaster in his arms!
Yet she has understanding of all tricks and turns,
just like a monkey. If they laugh, she doesn't mind.
Don't expect any good work done by her. She thinks
of only one thing, plans for one thing, all day long:
how she can do somebody else the biggest harm.

One from a bee. The man is lucky who gets her.
She is the only one no blame can settle on.
A man's life grows and blossoms underneath her touch.
She loves her husband, he loves her, and they grow old
together, while their glorious children rise to fame.
Among the throngs of other women this one shines
as an example. Heavenly grace surrounds her. She
alone takes no delight in sitting with the rest
when the conversation's about sex. It's wives like this
who are God's gift of happiness to mortal men.
These are the thoughtful wives, in every way the best.

But all those other breeds come to us too from God
and by his will. And they stay with us. They won't go.
For women are the biggest single bad thing Zeus
has made for us. Even when a wife appears to help,
her husband finds out in the end that after all
she didn't. No one day goes by from end to end
enjoyable, when you have spent it with your wife.
She will not stir herself to push the hateful god
Hard Times—that most unwelcome caller—out of doors.
At home, when a man thinks that, by God's grace or by
men's good will, there'll be peace for him and all go well,
she finds some fault with him and starts a fight. For where

there is a woman in the house, no one can ask
a friend to come and stay with him, and still feel safe.
Even the wife who appears to be the best-behaved
turns out to be the one who lets herself go wrong.
Her husband gawps and doesn't notice; neighbors do,
and smile to see how still another man gets fooled.
Each man will pick the faults in someone else's wife
and boast of his own each time he speaks of her. And yet
the same thing happens to us all. But we don't see.
For women are the biggest single bad thing Zeus
has made for us; a ball-and-chain; we can't get loose
since that time when the fight about a wife began
the Great War, and they volunteered, and went to hell.

2 · *The Vanity of Human Wishes*

My child, Zeus the deep-thundering holds the ends of all
actions in his own hands, disposes as he will
of everything. We who are human have no minds,
but live, from day to day, like beasts and nothing know
of what God plans to make happen to each of us.
But hope and self-persuasion keep us all alive
in our unprofitable desires. Some watch the day
for what it brings, and some the turn of years, and none
so downcast he will not believe that time to come
will make him virtuous, rich, all his heart's desire.
But other things begin to happen first; old age,
which no one wants, gets one before he makes his goal.
Painful diseases wear down some; others are killed
in battle, and death takes them under the dark earth.
Some, battered in the sudden hurricane on the sea,
where waves crowd big across the blue salt water, drown
and die, when all they looked for was some way to live.
Some loop (a dismal way to die) the noose around
their necks and go self-murdered from the sunlight. Thus
no evil thing is missing. In their thousands stand
bad spirits, and innumerable griefs, and pains
about our life. If men would take advice from me,
we should not long for what is really bad, nor buy
our heart's own torment for our hard work done in vain.

· 3 ·

The time of afterdeath for us is very long.
We live a wretched sum of years, and badly, too.

· 4 ·

No better thing befalls a man than a good wife,
no worse thing than a bad one.

· 5 ·

A woman thick around the ankles is no good.

HIPPONAX

Hermes, dear Hermes, Maia's son from Kylléne,
I pray to you, I'm suffering from extreme shivers,
so give an overcoat to Hippónax, give him
a cape, and sandals, and felt overshoes, sixty
pieces of gold to bury in his strong chamber.

TYRTAEUS

1 · *Courage: heros mortuus: heros vivus*

I would not say anything for a man nor take account of him
    for any speed of his feet or wrestling skill he might have,
not if he had the size of a Cyclops and strength to go with it,
    not if he could outrun Bóreas, the North Wind of Thrace,
not if he were more handsome and gracefully formed than Tithónos,
    or had more riches than Midas had, or Kínyras too,
not if he were more of a king than Tantalid Pelops,
    or had the power of speech and persuasion Adrastos had,

not if he had all splendors except for a fighting spirit.
　For no man ever proves himself a good man in war
unless he can endure to face the blood and the slaughter,
　go close against the enemy and fight with his hands.
Here is courage, mankind's finest possession, here is
　the noblest prize that a young man can endeavor to win,
and it is a good thing his city and all the people share with him
　when a man plants his feet and stands in the foremost spears
relentlessly, all thought of foul flight completely forgotten,
　and has well trained his heart to be steadfast and to endure,
and with words encourages the man who is stationed beside him.
　Here is a man who proves himself to be valiant in war.
With a sudden rush he turns to flight the rugged battalions
　of the enemy, and sustains the beating waves of assault.
And he who so falls among the champions and loses his sweet life,
　so blessing with honor his city, his father, and all his people,
with wounds in his chest, where the spear that he was facing has
　　transfixed
　　that massive guard of his shield, and gone through his breastplate
　　as well,
why, such a man is lamented alike by the young and the elders,
　and all his city goes into mourning and grieves for his loss.
His tomb is pointed to with pride, and so are his children,
　and his children's children, and afterward all the race that is his.
His shining glory is never forgotten, his name is remembered,
　and he becomes an immortal, though he lies under the ground,
when one who was a brave man has been killed by the furious War God
　standing his ground and fighting hard for his children and land.
But if he escapes the doom of death, the destroyer of bodies,
　and wins his battle, and bright renown for the work of his spear,
all men give place to him alike, the youth and the elders,
　and much joy comes his way before he goes down to the dead.
Aging, he has reputation among his citizens. No one
　tries to interfere with his honors or all he deserves;
all men withdraw before his presence, and yield their seats to him,
　the youth, and the men his age, and even those older than he.
Thus a man should endeavor to reach this high place of courage
　with all his heart, and, so trying, never be backward in war.

2 · *To the Soldiers, after a Defeat*

Now, since you are the seed of Herakles the invincible,
    courage! Zeus has not yet turned away from us. Do not
fear the multitude of their men, nor run away from them.
    Each man should bear his shield straight at the foremost ranks
and make his heart a thing full of hate, and hold the black flying
    spirits of death as dear as he holds the flash of the sun.
You know what havoc is the work of the painful War God,
    you have learned well how things go in exhausting war,
for you have been with those who ran and with the pursuers,
    O young men, you have had as much of both as you want.
Those who, standing their ground and closing their ranks together,
    endure the onset at close quarters and fight in the front,
they lose fewer men. They also protect the army behind them.
    Once they flinch, the spirit of the whole army falls apart.
And no man could count over and tell all the number of evils,
    all that can come to a man, once he gives way to disgrace.
For once a man reverses and runs in the terror of battle,
    he offers his back, a tempting mark to spear from behind,
and it is a shameful sight when a dead man lies in the dust there,
    driven through from behind by the stroke of an enemy spear.
No, no, let him take a wide stance and stand up strongly against them,
    digging both heels in the ground, biting his lip with his teeth,
covering thighs and legs beneath, his chest and his shoulders
    under the hollowed-out protection of his broad shield,
while in his right hand he brandishes the powerful war-spear,
    and shakes terribly the crest high above his helm.
Our man should be disciplined in the work of the heavy fighter,
    and not stand out from the missiles when he carries a shield,
but go right up and fight at close quarters and, with his long spear
    or short sword, thrust home and strike his enemy down.
Let him fight toe to toe and shield against shield hard driven,
    crest against crest and helmet on helmet, chest against chest;
let him close hard and fight it out with his opposite foeman,
    holding tight to the hilt of his sword, or to his long spear.
And you, O light-armed fighters, from shield to shield of your fellows
    dodge for protection and keep steadily throwing great stones,
and keep on pelting the enemy with your javelins, only
    remember always to stand near your own heavy-armed men.

SOLON

1 · *Prayer to the Muses*

Shining daughters of Memory and Zeus on Olympus,
  Muses, Piérides, listen to me in my prayers.
Grant me, at the hands of the blessed immortals, prosperity,
  and always a high degree in the opinion of men.
So shall I bring pleasure to friends and pain to my enemies,
  and my friends look on me in admiration, the others in fear.
My desire is to have riches; but win them unjustly
  I will not, for retribution must then come my way.
When it is gods who are giving it, wealth befalls a man as some
  solid plant, firm set from base of stock to the crest;
but cultivated with violence, it comes against nature,
  dragged and obedient under direction of crimes,
all unwilling it follows, and ruin is there in a moment.
  The beginning of disaster is not much, as when a fire
burns small in its first stages and ends in catastrophe. As fire's
  course is, such is the course taken by human misdeeds.
But Zeus forever is watching the end, and strikes of a sudden,
  as when a storm in spring abruptly scatters the clouds
and dredges up from the depth the open and heaving water
  where waves roll, and sweeping on across the generous land,
leaves in wreckage fair work men have done, till it hits the headlong
  sky, the gods' home, and the air is shining on every side
you look, and the blaze of the sun breaks out on the fertile acres
  in all its splendor, and there are no more clouds to be seen.
Such is the punishment Zeus gives, he does not, like a mortal,
  fall in a rage over each particular thing, and yet
it never escapes him all the way when a man has a sinful
  spirit; and always, in the end, his judgment is plain.
One man has to pay at once, one later, while others
  altogether escape overtaking by the gods' doom;
but then it always comes in aftertime, and the innocent
  pay, the sons of the sinners or those born long afterward.

But here is how we men, be we good, be we evil,
   think. Each keeps his own personal notion within
until he suffers. Then he cries out, but all until such time
   we take our idiot beguilement in light-weight hopes,
and one who is stricken and worn out in lingering sickness
   has taken measures and thinks he will grow healthy, and one
who is a coward expects to turn into a warlike hero.
   Another, ugly, thinks of the day when his looks will charm.
If one be penniless and sunk in the struggle of poverty,
   he, too, dreams upon the possession of huge estates.
They all rush off on their various business. One goes seafaring
   across the wide sea, in ships, where the fish swarm, trying to bring
a little money home, at the mercy of brutal hurricanes,
   no hard bargainer for his own life. While another, one
of those whose living is won by the bent plowshare and hard labor,
   furrows, year in year out, the tilth of his orchard ground.
One, who has learned Hephaistos' arts and the arts of Athene
   and all their skills, by work of his hands assembles a wage.
Yet another, dowered by the grace of Olympian Muses,
   has learned control of loveliness in the wisdom of verse.
One the lord far-ranging, Apollo, has made a soothsayer.
   He sees the evil coming from far away to a man
when the gods grant such knowledge; yet there is no way for bird sign
   nor sacrifice to ward off that which is fated to be.
Others, who understand the works of Paion with all his
   drugs, are healers. But neither are these complete in their craft,
seeing that often from a small pain grows a big affliction
   and no one, by giving mild remedies, can take it away,
while another, who is in agony from wasting afflictions,
   can suddenly be healed by a simple touch of the hand.
Fate brings humanity her good; she brings him her evil;
   and what the gods give us for gifts no man can refuse.
Danger, for all, lies in all action, and there is no telling
   which way the end will be after a thing is begun.
One may be trying to do well and, through failure of foresight,
   may fall into the curse of great disaster, while one
who acts badly may find God gives him all that he asked for,
   sheer good luck, that sets him free from the fault of his mind.
But money; there is no end of its making in human endeavor.

Those among us who have already the biggest estates
try to get twice as much as they have. Who can satisfy all of them?
   Money, when a man makes it, is the gift of the gods,
but disaster can grow out of money, and when retribution
   comes at the sending of Zeus, none can tell where it will light.

2 · *The Ten Ages of Man*

A child in his infancy grows his first set of teeth and loses them
   within seven years. For so long he counts as only a child.
When God has brought to accomplishment the next seven-year period,
   one shows upon his body the signs of maturing youth.
In the third period he is still getting his growth, while on his chin
   the beard comes, to show he is turning from youth to a man.
The fourth seven years are the time when every man reaches his
      highest
   point of physical strength where men look for prowess achieved.
In the fifth period the time is ripe for a young man
   to think of marriage and children, a family to be raised.
The mind of a man comes to full maturity in the sixth period,
   but he cannot now do as much, nor does he wish that he could.
In the seventh period of seven years and in the eighth also
   for fourteen years in all, his speech is best in his life.
He can still do much in his ninth period, but there is a weakening
   seen in his ability both to think and to speak.
But if he completes ten ages of seven years each, full measure,
   death, when it comes, can no longer be said to come too soon.

3 · *In Defense of His Policies*

My purpose was to bring my scattered people back
together. Where did I fall short of my design?
I call to witness at the judgment seat of time
one who is noblest, mother of Olympian
divinities, and greatest of them all, Black Earth.
I took away the mortgage stones stuck in her breast,
and she, who went a slave before, is now set free.
Into this sacred land, our Athens, I brought back
a throng of those who had been sold, some by due law,
though others wrongly; some by hardship pressed to escape

the debts they owed; and some of these no longer spoke
Attic, since they had drifted wide around the world,
while those in the country had the shame of slavery
upon them, and they served their masters' moods in fear.
These I set free; and I did this by strength of hand,
welding right law with violence to a single whole.
So have I done, and carried through all that I pledged.
I have made laws, for the good man and the bad alike,
and shaped a rule to suit each case, and set it down.
Had someone else not like myself taken the reins,
some ill-advised or greedy person, he would not
have held the people in. Had I agreed to do
what pleased their adversaries at that time, or what
they themselves planned to do against their enemies,
our city would have been widowed of her men. Therefore,
I put myself on guard at every side, and turned
among them like a wolf inside a pack of dogs.

MIMNERMUS

What, then, is life if love the golden is gone? What is pleasure?
    Better to die when the thought of these is lost from my heart:
the flattery of surrender, the secret embrace in the darkness.
    These alone are such charming flowers of youth as befall
women and men. But once old age with its sorrows advances
    upon us, it makes a man feeble and ugly alike,
heart worn thin with the hovering expectation of evil,
    lost all joy that comes out of the sight of the sun.
Hateful to boys a man goes then, unfavored of women.
    Such is the thing of sorrow God has made of old age.

THEOGNIS

· 19–26 ·

Kyrnos, this is my work; let a seal be stamped on the writing
  of these words, so that none who steals them shall ever deceive,
so that none in the presence of good work can substitute forgery.
  Thus shall each reader say: "These are the words of Theognis
of Megara, a great name, the world knows it." And yet
  I cannot please all the people in my own town.
No wonder there, son of Polypas, since not Zeus even
  can please all, by raining or withholding his rain.

· 39–52 ·

Kyrnos, this city is big with child, and I fear it will bring forth
  a man who will chastise all our disorderly ways.
The people in the city are still well behaved, but their leaders
  have turned their steps into a path that will make them corrupt.
Never yet, my Kyrnos, was a city destroyed by its nobles,
  but only after base men take to disorderly ways,
and debauch their own people and give rights to the unrighteous
  for the sake of their own money and power; and when this is so,
hold no hope for such a city to remain unshaken
  for long, although for the time it rides on a tranquil keel,
not when such activities have tempted the base men
  and private advantage comes with public disaster. For this
breeds civil discord and men's blood shed by their fellow-citizens,
  and monarchies. But pray that our city may never be such.

· 119–24 ·

Spurious gold and silver are an endurable evil,
  Kyrnos, and give no difficulty to the skilled man
to know what they are. But if the mind in a friend is secretly
  false and he carries a heart of trickery hidden within,
this, of all God's works among men, is the thing most spurious
  and most evil, since such deception can never be seen.

· 183–86 ·

Kyrnos, when we are breeding stock, we look for the best in
  horses, donkeys, or rams for stud, to get a good strain;
yet even the finest man is willing to marry a rascal's
  rascally daughter, if only she brings him money enough.

· 237–54 ·

See, I have given you wings on which to hover uplifted
  high above earth entire and the great waste of the sea
without strain. Wherever men meet in festivals, as men
  gather, you will be there, your name will be spoken again
as the young singers, with the flutes clear piping beside them,
  make you into a part of the winsome verses, and sing
of you. And even after you pass to the gloom and the secret
  chambers of sorrow, Death's house hidden under the ground,
even in death your memory shall not pass, and it shall not
  die, but always, a name and a song in the minds of men,
Kyrnos, you shall outrange the land of Greece and the islands,
  cross the upheaving sea where the fish swarm, carried not
astride the back of a horse, but the shining gifts of the dark-wreathed
  Muses shall be the force that carries you on your way.
For all wherever song is you shall be there for the singers.
  So long as earth endures and sun endures, you shall be.
I did this. But you give me not the smallest attention.
  You put me off with deceits as if I were a little child.

· 667–82 ·

If I had money, Simonides, as I have had in time past,
  I could without embarrassment consort with the great.
But as it is, I know a man, and he passes me by. Dumb
  stand I, for poverty, though I know as much as the rest
even now. So it is. We are swept with the wind, white sails lost,
  out from the Melian Sea, on into the gloom of the night.
The men are unwilling to bail any more. The sea washes over
  the bulwarks on either side, and barely and in distress
we keep afloat. But some are at work. They have put down the noble
  helmsman, who knew his business well, and kept a good watch.

All discipline is gone, and they plunder the cargo at random,
  nor is there any fair division made for the lot.
The base hands and the porters control, the great are beneath them.
  I am afraid. I think the sea will swallow our ship.
Let this be my secret cipher addressed to the nobles;
  but even the base man, if he is clever, can see what it means.

· 699–718 ·

For the multitude of mankind there is only one virtue:
  Money. And there was no good found in anything else,
not if you had the sagacity of the great Rhadamánthys,
  not if you had the resource of Sísyphos, Aíolos' son,
who by the crafty guile in his mind came up out of Hades
  and flattered the Queen of the Dead into letting him go,
Persephone, who dims men's mind with the water of Lethe;
  and to this day no other man has made such an escape,
once the darkness of death has closed in a vapor about him,
  once he has taken his way to the shadowy place of the dead
and gone on through the black gates which shut the protesting
  souls of dead men in and will not let them go free;
yet Sísyphos was a hero who came back even from that place
  into the light of the sun through the resource in his mind;
not if you could be false and make falsehood look like honesty,
  not if you had fair speech like Nestor the almost-divine,
not if in the speed of your feet you outran the flying
  Harpies or the North Wind's two sons in the storm of their feet.
None of these; but all men must understand when I tell them:
  Money, and nothing but Money, holds all the power in the world.

· 869–72 ·

May wide and towering heaven collapse upon me in all its
  bronze and terror, catastrophe to the peoples of earth,
on that day when I no longer stand by my companions,
  on that day when I cease to harry my enemies.

ALCMAN

Maiden Song

There is vengeance from the gods.
Blessed is the man who blithely
winds out all his day of life
without tears. But I must sing the
light of Ágido. I see her
like the sun that Ágido
summons up to shine upon us.
But our lovely choir leader
will not let me praise her, or
say she is not fair.
Well she knows that she herself is
something dazzling
just as if among a herd of
cattle one should set a racehorse,
sinewy, swift, and with feet full of thunder,
creature out of a dream with wings.

Look and see. That other is
like a fleet Venetian courser,
but the tresses of my cousin
Hagesíchora! They blossom
into gold without alloy,
and her face is pale like silver.
Must I tell you this so plainly?
There is Hagesíchora.
Loveliest after Ágido,
she will still run,
Lydian horse with Scythian racer
close together;
for the Pleiades against us,
as we carry Órthria's plow
through the divine night, rise up to strive
    with us,
blazing bright as a single star.

Luxury of purple dye,
all we have can never help us,
not the carven bracelet-snake,
not the wimple sheer in gold
Lydian, the pride and glory
of the girls with delicate eyes,
not the hair of Nanno, not
Áreta's immortal beauty,
never Kleasísera,
not Thúlakis,
nor go to Ainesímbrota's
house and say:
Let Ástaphis be on my side;
let Philýlla look my way;
give me Damáreta, lovely Iánthemis.
Hagesíchora is all our hope.

Does not Hagesíchora
with the lovely ankles, help us?
Does she wait with Ágido?
Does she praise our festival?
But you gods, accept their prayers,
for the end and the achievement
come from God. My chorus leader,
maiden as I am, I say
I have only shrilled in vain
from the roof tops
like an owl; yet I would also
please our Lady
of the Dawn; for it was she who
came to heal us of our trouble.
Maidens, we have come to the peace desired,
all through Hagesíchora's grace.

All the chariot's course is swung
to the running of the trace-horse,
all the ship must come to heel,
swiftly to the captain's handling.
She has sung her song today

not more sweetly than the sirens
(they are gods). But how we sang,
we ten girls instead of the Eleven!
One is trilling like a swan by
Xanthos river,
one with splendid tawny hair. . . .

IBYCUS

In spring time the Kydonian
quinces, watered by running streams,
there where the maiden nymphs have
their secret garden, and grapes that grow
round in shade of the tendriled vine,
ripen.
      Now in this season for me
there is no rest from love.
Out of the hard bright sky,
a Thracian north wind blowing
with searing rages and hurt—dark,
pitiless, sent by Aphrodite—Love
rocks and tosses my heart.

STESICHORUS

1 · *Helen and Klytaimestra*

So once, when Tyndareus
made sacrifices to all the gods, he forgot one only, the giver of blessings,
Aphrodite. And she in anger
with the daughters of Tyndareus made them twice married and three
    times married
and brides who deserted their husbands.

2 · *Palinode to Helen*

That story is not true.
You never sailed in the benched ships.
You never went to the city of Troy.

SAPPHO

1 · *Invocation to Aphrodite*

Throned in splendor, deathless, O Aphrodite,
child of Zeus, charm-fashioner, I entreat you
not with griefs and bitternesses to break my
        spirit, O goddess;

standing by me rather, if once before now
far away you heard, when I called upon you,
left your father's dwelling place and descended,
        yoking the golden

chariot to sparrows, who fairly drew you
down in speed aslant the black world, the bright air
trembling at the heart to the pulse of countless
        fluttering wingbeats.

Swiftly then they came, and you, blessed lady,
smiling on me out of immortal beauty,
asked me what affliction was on me, why I
        called thus upon you,

what beyond all else I would have befall my
tortured heart: "Whom then would you have Per-
    suasion
force to serve desire in your heart? Who is it,
        Sappho, that hurt you?

Though she now escape you, she soon will follow;
though she take not gifts from you, she will give
    them:
though she love not, yet she will surely love you
        even unwilling."

In such guise come even again and set me
free from doubt and sorrow; accomplish all those
things my heart desires to be done; appear and
      stand at my shoulder.

· 2 ·

Like the very gods in my sight is he who
sits where he can look in your eyes, who listens
close to you, to hear the soft voice, its sweetness
      murmur in love and

laughter, all for him. But it breaks my spirit;
underneath my breast all the heart is shaken.
Let me only glance where you are, the voice dies,
      I can say nothing,

but my lips are stricken to silence, underneath my skin the tenuous flame suffuses;
nothing shows in front of my eyes, my ears are
      muted in thunder.

And the sweat breaks running upon me, fever
shakes my body, paler I turn than grass is;
I can feel that I have been changed, I feel that
      death has come near me.

· 3 ·

Some there are who say that the fairest thing seen
on the black earth is an array of horsemen;
some, men marching; some would say ships; but I say
      she whom one loves best

is the loveliest. Light were the work to make this
plain to all. Since she who surpassed in beauty
all mortality beside, Helen, chose that
      man as the noblest

who destroyed the glory of Troy entirely.
Not the thought of child, nor beloved parents,
was remembered, after the Queen of Cyprus
      won her at first sight.

Since young brides have hearts that can be persuaded
easily, light things, palpitant to passion
as am I, remembering Anaktória
    who has gone from me

and whose lovely walk and the shining pallor
of her face I would rather see before my
eyes than Lydia's chariots in all their glory
    armored for battle.

4 · *To a Rival*

You will die and be still, never shall be memory left of you
after this, nor regret when you are gone. You have not touched the
    flowers
of the Muses, and thus, shadowy still in the domain of Death,
you must drift with a ghost's fluttering wings, one of the darkened
    dead.

· 5 ·

But I claim there will be some who remember us when we are gone.

· 6 ·

When we lived all as one, she adored you as
symbol of some divinity,
Arignóta, delighted in your dancing.

Now she shines among Lydian women as
into dark when the sun has set
the moon, pale-handed, at last appeareth

making dim all the rest of the stars, and light
spreads afar on the deep, salt sea,
spreading likewise across the flowering cornfields;

and the dew rinses glittering from the sky;
roses spread, and the delicate
antherisk, and the lotus spreads her petals.

So she goes to and fro there, remembering
Atthis and her compassion, sick
the tender mind, and the heart with grief is eaten.

7 · *Epitaph*

This is the dust of Timas, who died before she was married
and whom Persephone's dark chamber accepted instead.
After her death the maidens who were her friends, with sharp iron
cutting their lovely hair, laid it upon her tomb.

ALCAEUS

1 · *Storm in the State*

I cannot understand how the winds are set
against each other. Now from this side and now
    from that the waves roll. We between them
      run with the wind in our black ship driven,

hard pressed and laboring under the giant storm.
All round the mast-step washes the sea we shipped.
    You can see through the sail already
      where there are opening rents within it.

The forestays slacken. . . .

    Now jettison all cargo; ride out
      best as we can in the pounding surf beat.

They say that, beaten hard by the running seas,
the ship herself no longer will fight against
    the wildness of the waves, would rather
      strike on the reefs underneath, and founder.

2 · *Prayer for Safety at Sea*

Be with me now, leaving the Isle of Pelops,
mighty sons of Zeus and of Leda, now in
kindliness of heart appear to me, Kastor
    and Polydeúkes:

you who wander over the wide earth, over
all the sea's domain on your flying horses,
easily delivering mortal men from
    death and its terror:

swept in far descent to the strong-built vessel's
masthead, you ride shining upon the cables,
through the weariness of the dark night bringing
    light to the black ship.

3 · *Winter Scene*

Zeus rains upon us, and from the sky comes down
enormous winter. Rivers have turned to ice. . . .

Dash down the winter. Throw a log on the fire
and mix the flattering wine (do not water it
    too much) and bind on round our foreheads
    soft ceremonial wreaths of spun fleece.

We must not let our spirits give way to grief.
By being sorry we get no further on,
    my Bukchis. Best of all defenses
    is to mix plenty of wine, and drink it.

· 4 ·

Wet your whistle with wine now, for the dog star, wheeling up the
    sky,
brings back summer, the time all things are parched under the sear-
    ing heat.
Now the cicada's cry, sweet but too long, shrills from beneath the
    leaves.
Now the artichoke flowers, women are lush, ask too much of their
    men,
who grow lank, for the star burning above withers their brains and
    knees.

ANACREON

· 1 ·

The love god with his golden curls
puts a bright ball into my hand,
shows a girl in her fancy shoes,
    and suggests that I take her.

Not that girl—she's the other kind,
one from Lesbos. Disdainfully,
nose turned up at my silver hair,
    she makes eyes at the ladies.

· 2 ·

Once he went out huddled about in dirty clothes with his hair skimped
    up,
buttons of wood hung in his ears for rings, and the hide of a thread-
    bare ox
scrubbed from a cast-off shield to wrap
his bones to keep him warm. For friends all he could get was pastry
    cooks
or girls who walked the streets for fun. He was the lousy Ártemon.
He lived the life of a useless bum.
He got his neck framed in the pillory, he got whipped till his back
    was raw,
he had hairs pulled out of his head.
Look at him now, Kýkē's boy; he rides in a coach and four, and wears
gold on his arms, gold on his neck, shaded by ivory parasols,
like some dame in society.

ANONYMOUS DRINKING SONGS

· 1 ·

I will wear my sword in a spray of myrtle
like Harmódios and Aristogeíton
when they killed the usurper and made
Athens be once again a city where all are free.

Dear Harmódios, surely you have not perished.
No, they say, you live in the blessed islands
where Achilles, the swift of foot,
and Tydeus' son, Diomedes, are said to have gone.

I will wear my sword in a spray of myrtle
like Harmódios and Aristogeíton
when at Athene's processional
they killed Hippárchos, the man who had usurped
    the power.

Always your fame shall live with us forever,
dear Harmódios and Aristogeíton,
since you killed the usurper and made
Athens be once again a city where all are free.

· 2 ·

He who never betrays one he has made a friend shall be given high
exaltation among people and gods. Such is my own belief.

· 3 ·

Oh that it were given to us to open
up the heart of every man, and to read his
mind within, and then to close it,
and thus, never deceived, be assured of a friend.

· 4 ·

Underneath every stone there lies hidden a scorpion, dear friend.
Take care, or he will sting you. All concealment is treachery.

SIMONIDES

1 · *Danae and Perseus*

. . . when in the wrought chest
the wind blowing over
and the sea heaving
struck her with fear, her cheeks not dry,
she put her arm over Perseus and spoke: My child
such trouble I have.
And you sleep, your heart is placid;
you dream in the joyless wood;
in the night nailed in bronze,
in the blue dark you lie still and shine.
The salt water that towers above your head
as the wave goes by you
heed not, nor the wind's voice; you press
your bright face to the red blanket.
If this danger were danger to you,
your small ear would attend my words.
But I tell you: Sleep, my baby, and let the sea sleep, let
our trouble sleep; let some change appear

Zeus father, from you.
This bold word and beyond justice
I speak, I pray you, forgive it me.

2 · *Comment on a Poem of Cleobúlus*

The Epitaph of Cleobúlus

I am the maiden in bronze set over the tomb of Midas.
As long as water runs from wellsprings, and tall trees burgeon,
and the sun goes up the sky to shine, and the moon is brilliant,
as long as rivers shall flow and the wash of the sea's breakers,
so long remaining in my place on this tomb where the tears fall
I shall tell those who pass that Midas here lies buried.

The Comment of Simonides

Who that trusts his mind could believe the man of Lindos, Cleobúlus,
who against the forever flow of rivers, the spring flowers,
against sun's flame and moon gold
and the tossing of the sea, sets up the strength of a gravestone?
All things are less than the gods. That stone
even a man's hand could smash. This is the word of a fool.

· 3 ·

Being no more than a man, you cannot tell what will happen tomor-
    row,
nor, when you see one walk in prosperity know for how much time
    it will be.
For overturn on the light-lifting wings of a dragonfly
is not more swift.

· 4 ·

Not even those who lived long ago before us
and were sons of our lords, the gods, themselves half-divine,
came to an old age and the end of their days
without hardship and danger, nor did they live forever.

· 5 ·

There is one story
that Virtue has her dwelling place above rock walls hard to climb
with a grave chorus of light-footed nymphs attendant about her,
and she is not to be looked upon by the eyes of every mortal,
only by one who with sweat, with clenched concentration
and courage, climbs to the peak.

· 6 ·

To be a good man, without blame and without question,
foursquare founded hand and foot, mind also
faultless fashioned, is difficult.

Thus the word of Pittakos, but it does not
run right, though it was a wise man who said it:

that it is difficult to be excellent. Not difficult;
only a god could have this privilege; it is not *possible*
for a man not to go bad
when he has more bad luck than he can handle.
Any man is good while his luck is good,
bad when bad, and for the most part they are best
whom the gods love.

Therefore, I will not throw away my time and life
into unprofitable hope and emptiness, the search
for that object which cannot possibly be,
the Utterly Blameless Man among all of us who enjoy
man's food on the wide earth.
But if I find one, I will let you know.
No, I admire all, am a friend of any
who of his own will does nothing shameful. Against
necessity not even the gods can fight.

I do not like to find fault.
Enough for me if one is not
bad, not too unsteady, knows
what is right and good for his city,
a sound man. I will not
look out his faults. For the generation
of fools is endless. Take anything as good
which is not soiled with shame.

· 7 ·

Across the pale stillness
of water keel-carven, these lovely eyes of desire
drag the ship to her doom.

· 8 ·

As when in the winter moons God stills
weather a space of fourteen days,
and winds sleep in the season, and men have named it
sacred to the breeding of the bright halcyon.

INSCRIBED EPITAPHS

· 9 ·

Traveler, take this word to the men of Lakedaímon:
We who lie buried here did what they told us to do.

· 10 ·

This is the grave of that Megístias, whom once the Persians
and Medes killed when they crossed Spercheíos River; a seer
who saw clearly the spirits of death advancing upon him,
yet could not bring himself to desert the Spartiate kings.

· 11 ·

Friend, we once were alive in the harbor city of Korinth.
Now the island city of Salamis is our grave.

PINDAR

O Thrasyboúlos, I send this gear of racing and lovely
songs to you for the end of your revels. So may you share it
with them who drink beside you, sweet instigator to them,
    to the yield

of Dionysos' abundance and the flagons of Athens
at that time of night when the troublesome cares of humanity
drift from our hearts and on seas of luxury streaming in gold

we swim together, and make for a shore that is nowhere.
The poor man now is rich. . . .

BACCHYLIDES

1 · *The Coming of Theseus: A Dithyramb*

Chorus with leader

King of Athens, the sacred city,
lord of luxurious Ionians,
what news of war is this that the trumpet's
bronze-belled braying call announces?
Is it some enemy war captain
overstriding our land's boundaries
with his own host at heel?
Is it robbers, whose ways are evil,
overcoming our shepherds' resistance,
driving our flocks away?
What is it that gnaws at your heart?
Tell us; for I think, if any man
has the strong support of hard-fighting
men-at-arms, it is you,
O son of Pandíon and Kreoúsa, Aígeus.

King of Athens

A messenger has come in, completing
the long run between here and the Isthmus,
telling of deeds incredible done by
a strong man. He has killed overpowering
Sinis, once the greatest in strength
of men, being son to Kronid Lytaíos
(earthshaker, that is, Poseidon);
killed, too, the manslaughtering wild boar
in the valley of Krémmyon, and killed
wicked and cruel Skiron.
He has abolished the wrestling-ring
of Kérkyon. The Pounder has dropped
Polypémon's strong hammer from hand.

« 35 »

He met with a better man. I fear
this news. I do not know what it all may come to.

Chorus with leader

Who is this hero, then, does he say?
Where does he come from? What has he with him?
Does he come armed with weapons of war?
Has he a great following behind him?
Or alone, and with body servants
only, goes he as a merchant who travels
into alien lands?
Strong he must be, and resolute,
adventurous, too, who has stood the onset
of such big men and put them down.
Surely, the drive of a god is behind him,
to bring law to the lawless people.
It is no easy thing to engage
again and again, and never be loser.
In the length of time all things are brought to com-
    pletion.

King of Athens

The man says only two attendants
go with him. On his gleaming shoulders
he wears a sword with an ivory hilt;
two polished throwing-spears in his hands;
a well-wrought skin-cap of Sparta
covers his head and his bright hair;
over his chest a sea-dyed
shirt, and, above, a Thessalian
cloak of frieze. In his eyes there shines
the flamelight of a Lemnos
volcano. Yet he is said to be
a boy, in his first youth, but a boy
trained to feel the finesse of war
and bronze-battering Ares' work.
The end of his search is said to be shining Athens.

2 · *Olympian Ode for Híeron* (*Horse Race*)

High lord and leader of men
in Syracuse of the dashing horses,
you shall be judge of this work
of art, this gift of the violet-wreathed Muses, you,
if any man on earth,
can read it. Rest then that just
mind, stilled now, undisturbed by troubles,
turn our way your deep attention,
if by consent of the deep-waisted goddesses of Grace
your far friend in his sacred
island fashioned and sent
to your famous city this song
which he, a great servant of gold-veiled
Urania, made. His wish is
that the voice spring from within him

in praise of Híeron. Shearing
the deep sky with his golden pinions
and high speed of wings,
the eagle, messenger to the wide majesty
of Zeus loud-thundering,
goes bold in his big strength, and below
the thin-screaming small birds
huddle away from him, in fear.
Not the lifted peaks of great earth are barrier,
not the harsh climbing crests
of ever heaving salt water. Out
in lone space he steers
the glossed and light plumes of his wings
and rides the west wind
to fill the eyes of men with wonder.

Like him, I too have a thousand ways to go for my
        choosing
for the song of your achievement
given by the hands of Victory, lady of the dark tresses,
by armor-chested Ares also,
you lordly sons of Deinómenes.

May the god who uses you well not weary of it.
Dawn, goddess, she of the golden arms
looked down and saw the bay horse, Pherénikos,
run like a storm by the broad
whirling waters of Alpheos river to win his race.

So too in hallowed Pytho.
I lean hand on earth and declare,
never yet have rival horses
run before him, the dust of them fouling him as he
    galloped
down the home stretch to his goal.
He goes like a gust of the north wind,
yet waits the will of his rider, to sweep
fresh victories for Híeron
and bursts of applause for that hospitable man.
Fortunate he, whom the god
has granted his share of splendors,
and, with that happiness all wish for,
to go through a prosperous lifetime: not
blessed in everything: for no man
born has fortune on his side always.

No, for there was a time,
the legends say, when even the invincible
son of white-thunder-flashing
Zeus, Herakles, went down to the dark gates of
    light-footed
Persephone, to haul up
that jag-toothed dog whom the snaky monster
spawned, from death to daylight.
There, beside the Waters of Wailing,
he was aware of the ghosts of unhappy dead men
rustling, as on the colored slopes
of Ida, where the flocks are pastured,
wind stirs the leaves. Clear showed
among them the shade of Meleágros,
Portheus' grandson, in his day a daring
man at arms with the handled spear.

Now as Alkméne's strong and glorious son saw
    Meleágros
shining in all his war gear,
he hooked the loud twanging string to the bowhorn,
then plucked a brazen-headed arrow,
flipping the quiver-lid
back. But facing him now the phantom of Meleágros
came closer, and knew him well,
and, knowing him, spoke: "Son of Zeus,
the great god, hold fast
where you are, and pacify that adventurous spirit.

Useless for you to let fly
from your hands a rasping arrow
into the ghosts of dead men.
You have nothing to fear." He spoke. Amphítryon's
    lordly
son stared at him in wonder,
answered: "What immortal god,
or was it a mortal, raised such a branch
of strength? What country could breed such?
Who could have killed you? Surely then Hera, girt in
    splendor,
will send your killer to hunt
my head too. But Pallas Athene,
the golden-haired, will be there to help me."
Then bursting into tears, Meleágros
answered him: "It is hard for men
who are mere earthly creatures to fend off

what the gods have determined to do.
Otherwise Oíneus, lasher of horses,
would have turned back the rancor of Artemis,
the white-armed, the high goddess with buds of flow-
    ers in her hair,
with supplication by abundant
sacrifice of goats and of red-backed
oxen. He was my father.

No, but
the goddess kept her anger untamed
and would not let be. The Maiden let loose a powerful,
cruelly fighting wild boar
on the lordly countryside of Kalydon.
There, in swelled riptide of brute force,
he tore with tusks the poled vineyards,
slaughtered the sheep flocks and any man
who dared stand his ground against him.

Around this creature we, the chosen best out of all
the Hellenes,
closed in and fought with a will
six whole days on end, till at last the goddess
let us men of Aitolia win.
We buried those who had gone down
before the onrush and screaming charge of the wild
boar,
Ankaíos and with him Ageláos,
bravest of all my excellent brothers,
born in the same renowned palace
with me to Althaía and to Oíneus our father.

With these, sorrowful fate destroyed
others also. For Artemis, Leto's proud daughter,
had not yet made an end
to the cruelty of her anger, and over the warm-colored
hide
we now fought on with a will,
we and the battling Kourétes.
There, with many more beside,
I myself killed Íphiklos
and great Áphares, my mother's quick-fighting brothers. See you,
the war god, reckless in anger,
knows not friend from foe in the fighting.
Bolts are thrown blind from our hands
against the lives of all fighting against us,

and the flown spear brings death
to all against whom the god directs it.

The proud daughter of Thestios,
who (to my sorrow) was my mother,
did not take this into account,
but plotted my death. A pitiless woman she.
She took from its carven box
and broke and burned the log, soon gone,
which fate at my birth had designed
to be the measure of my own life,
lost with my death, I lost with it. I was then
in the very act of plundering
the strong body of Daípylos' son
Klýmenos, caught before the walls
where our enemies had fled away
to the ancient and strong-founded city

Pleuron. Little was the sweetness of life I had left
    then.
I felt the strength going from me,
ah, and with tears, in sorrow the last of my breathing,
the young force gone and the glory."
They say that Amphítryon's son
who never feared battlecry, then, that only time
felt eyes fill with tears, in pity
over that much-suffering man
and spoke to him in answer
thus: "Better for mortals never to come into existence,

never to look on the sun's shining.
Still, seeing there will be no advantage
got for us in mourning these matters,
we should put our minds to that which we may get done.
Could it be that within the halls
of Oíneus, the beloved of Ares,
there is among his unwedded daughters
one whose beauty is like your own?
Such a one I could wish to take as my shining bride."

To him now the spirit
of battle-brave Meleágros answered:
"I left behind in the house
Deïaneíra, her throat still green
with youth, and innocent still
of love, and the charms love can work on the flesh."

White-armed Lady of Legend, Kallíope,
bring to a halt your compact chariot
here. Sing Zeus, the son of Kronos,
Olympian god and lord of the gods on Olympos;
sing the unwearied surging river
Álpheos; sing the strength of Pelops;
Pisa the meadow where the glorious
horse Pherénikos won his race,
outfooting all, and back to the strong walls of Syracuse,
back to Híeron brought returning
the leafed branch of high success.
For grace and sake of truth it becomes us
to give praise, and with both hands push
rancorous spite away, when
any man does well and prospers.

Such was the gracious saying of the great Boiotian,
Hesiod, the close follower
of the Muses: "When the immortal gods set a man
        high,
let men's fame be given him also."
Lightly will I obey,
turn no inch from the course but let my lips' acclama-
        tion
be conveyed to Híeron. Thence
grow the stocks of excellent plants
which may Zeus, the great gardener,
keep in stillness of peace, untroubled forever.

3 · *Olympian Ode for Híeron* (*Chariot Race*)

Of Demeter, queen of most fruitful Sicily,
with her daughter, Maiden of the violet

garland, sing, Kleio, dispenser of sweetness,
sing for Olympic fields the speed of Híeron's

horses, who ran with towering success beside them;
with glory there beside the broad-whirling stream
of Álpheos they made Deinómenes' prospering
son the winner of garlands, and the uncounted

multitude cried in his honor:
"Ah, thrice fortunate this man
who from Zeus's own hand bestowed
with highest privilege of place
among Hellenes, knows how to keep his tower-piled
      wealth
clear of the hiding sheath of darkness."

Streets are alive with festal sacrifices
of oxen, alive with entertainment of friends
from far. High wrought and shining with gold, the
      gleam
plays from tripods set in a row before

the temple, where the greatest of groves is sacred
to Phoebus by the Kastalian stream, and men
of Delphoi served him. Let the God be glorified,
God, for over fortunes his power is greatest.

There was a time the lord of horse-taming
Lydia saw destined things
come to pass, saw Zeus's decree
fulfilled and brought to an end
when Sardeis fell to the horde of the Persians, only
Apollo, he of the golden sword,

guarded and kept him. Now Croesus came to the day
      of tears
unhoped for and had no mind to endure
slavery still, but let build a pyre
before the bronze-nailed wall of his courtyard

and there with his gracious wife ascended
and with his daughters of the braided hair, who wept

and mourned incessantly. Then Croesus lifted
his hands, and theirs, to the steep air

and spoke: "O powerful spirit,
where is the gratitude of gods?
Where is the king who is Leto's son?
The house of Alyáttes is fallen,
and nothing befalls me for all the thousand treasures
I had conveyed to him before,

no, but the aged citadel of the Lydians
burns, and Paktólos' gold-spinning waters
run red with blood, our wives are led forth
from their strong secret houses in shame.

All that I hated before is sweet now. Best to die."
So he spoke, and caused a soft-stepping attendant
to light the piled wood. The maidens his daughters
    broke out
in tears, and stretched their hands to their mother,

for to mortals the death seen coming
is bitterest of all ways to die.
But now, as the shining power
of the flames' menace burst high,
it was Zeus who drove a cloud's dark sheathing
above them and drenched the yellow flame.

Nothing passes belief when a god's intention
wills it. So Delian-born Apollo
carried off to the land of the Hyperboréans
the ancient, settled him there with his light-foot
    daughters, because

he was pious, because beyond all other
mortals he gave gifts to sacred Pytho.
So he. Of those now in Hellas, there is none,
O Híeron high in praise, who will venture

to say any man has given more
gold to Loxias than you. Therefore,
the man who fattens not on rancor
can readily speak praise of one

whom God loves, who loves horses, a man of battles,
who holds scepter from Zeus of the laws,

who holds place from the violet-wreathed Muses,
whose own hand was terrible once in war,
though now, in old age, you look on the day's blessing
quietly, and know it will not be long.

Still, hope is treacherous, she hides under the hearts
of us who are mortal. The lord of oracles,
Apollo, said to the son of Pheres:
"You are mortal. Best to have two predictions

in hand. Think to see tomorrow's
sun, and no sun thereafter.
Think to live for fifty years
through in deep-based wealth to the end.
Do your duties, so win your pleasure. Here lies
advantage higher than all."

I speak to one who can follow me. The deep
of the sky stains not. The water of the sea
is not dirtied with rot. Gold fights tarnish.
But it is not allowed for a man to pass

where age is gray, and then once more recover
strong youth. Yet there is no diminution
in man's good, his light, as the body goes. Still
the Muse sustains him. Híeron, you have shown out

the greatest splendors in flowers of wealth
before men. If one does well,
not silence brings his appropriate
glory. And with his honors here remembered,
men shall sound out too the exquisite grace
of me, the nightingale of Keos.

ANONYMOUS GOLD BURIAL TABLET

You will find to the left of the house of Hades a wellspring,
and by the side of this standing a white cypress.
You must not even go close to this wellspring; but also
you will find another spring that comes from the lake of Memory,
cold water running, and there are those who stand guard before it.
You shall say: "I am a child of earth and the starry heavens,
but my generation is of the sky. You yourselves know this.
But I am dry with thirst and am dying. Give me then quickly
the water that runs cold out of the lake of Memory."
And they themselves will give you to drink from the sacred water,
and afterward you shall be lord among the rest of the heroes.

NOTES, CHIEFLY BIOGRAPHICAL

Archilochus

Probable dates about 680–640 B.C. Born at Paros to a Parian aristocrat and a slave woman. Helped with the new foundation of Thasos. A soldier of fortune and amateur poet.

Numbers 1–7 seem to me to be, not fragments, but very short complete poems. It has been doubted whether Archilochus really wrote Nos. 5 and 23.

Callínus

Active in the middle of the seventh century. The invasion he mentions seems to be that of the Cimmerian barbarians. Callinus came from Ephesos in Asia Minor.

Semónides

The spelling of his name is not certain, but this form helps distinguish him from the later (and greater) Simonides. From the little Aegean island of Amorgos. Date quite uncertain; perhaps late seventh century. Practically nothing is known of his life.

Hippónax

Of Ephesos. Sixth century, apparently, but little is known about him, and little of his work remains. He invented the *choliambic* or "lame iambic," reversing the stress at the end of the line so as to bring the reader down hard on the wrong foot. Very talented, but colloquial, difficult, sparsely preserved.

Tyrtaéus

Active at Sparta, probably late in the seventh century. He may have been a Spartan, an Athenian, or a Milesian—most probably the last—and invited into Sparta as an expert who could inspire the soldiers to military virtue. A rather tiresome poet, but not always inept.

Solon

The great and good Athenian social reformer and the first literary man at Athens about whom we know anything. His long life may have extended from about 630 to 550 B.C.

Mimnérmus

Of Colophon, in Asia Minor. Apparently an older contemporary of Solon, thus living perhaps in the later seventh and early sixth centuries.

Theógnis

Alone among the poets here represented (except Pindar), Theognis survives not in fragments but in a manuscript of his own. This, however, has produced its own puzzle. What we have is a long series of elegies, of varying lengths, running to nearly 1,400 lines. This contains, usually with slight variations, poems elsewhere ascribed to Tyrtaeus, Mimnermus, and Solon, and it suggests that the work of Theognis himself may have formed the basis for some sort of anthology. Lines 19–26 obviously bear on this problem, but do nothing to solve it. In my own opinion, only the selections here included which are addressed to Kyrnos are the work of Theognis, the others doubtful.

Theognis himself came from Megara, lived in the middle or later sixth century, and may have lasted on into the fifth. The poems in this collection had a demonstrably strong influence on Athenian writers, particularly Euripides and Plato.

Alcman

Sometimes thought, from a reference in his own writing, to have been a Lydian, but more probably a Spartan. In any case, he wrote choral lyric at Sparta, probably in the second half of the seventh century. His one large fragment, for a choir of Spartan girls competing at a festival, has charmed and puzzled readers since the papyrus was first published. Text and interpretation raise one problem after another. I give it here in an old translation which I have not been able to improve much, for whatever it may offer.

Íbycus

Born, it seems, at Rhegium, a Greek colony in Italy. Active in the second half of the sixth century. One of the earliest of the professional poets who traveled from city to city and made a good living out of choral composition.

Stesíchorus

Another western Greek poet, from southern Italy or Sicily; a wandering professional, apparently, whose name suggests that choral lyric was traditional in his family. His identity is obscure; there may have been more than one early Stesichorus, but these fragments probably come from the early or middle sixth century. Stesichorus was a master of the long, narrative lyric; his influence on Attic tragedy may have been very great, but his fragments are meager. As to Helen, the story goes that he was blinded for slandering that heroine (or goddess), apologized, and regained his sight.

Sappho

Of Mytilene on the island of Lesbos. Lived apparently from the late seventh century well into the sixth. Her specialty was short lyrics, for a single reciter or private reading, in the dialect of her own country and in simple but superbly articulated stanzas. Best known, but not exclusively, for love poems. Of these selections, No. 3 is a much-reconstructed piece, and the authenticity of the middle part cannot be guaranteed. It has also been reasonably questioned whether she really wrote No. 7, the "Epitaph for Timas."

Alcaéus

Countryman and contemporary (perhaps a little younger) of Sappho. He lived a stormy youth as an aristocrat resisting social reform in his city. Politically, he may illustrate the kind of group Solon had to contend with, or Solon's counterpart at Lesbos, the enlightened Pittakos. As a craftsman in verse, however, he rivals Sappho at her best.

Anácreon

Driven from Teos, his Asia Minor home, by the Persian inroad, he settled with his countrymen in Thrace and later pursued a career as a professional poet, ending his days perhaps in Athens. He lived from, perhaps, about 560 to 490 B.C.

He is more important for his influence than for his own surviving work. The far later *Anacreontea*, which were never meant to pass as anything but frank imitations of Anacreon, had an immense influence on the lyric of the Renaissance.

Simónides

Of Keos, a small independent island in the Aegean. Supposed to have lived from 556 to about 468 B.C. A widely traveled and widely known professional, friend of the great generals, at home in both Athens and Sparta and, it seems, anywhere in Greece, he was, above all, the poet of Pan-Hellenic resistance against the great Persian invasion of 480 B.C. One of the wisest and certainly the most versatile of all Greek lyric poets.

The ascription of No. 6 to Simonides is uncertain. So also is that of No. 9; but we know that Simonides did write in commemoration of Leonidas and the Spartans who died at Thermopylae.

Bacchýlides

Nephew of Simonides, contemporary and rival of Pindar (who lived from 518 to about 440 B.C.). Number 1 is a complete, short dithyramb, or dramatic lyric; the others are victory odes in the manner made familiar by Pindar. For text and interpretation, I am particularly indebted to Edmonds, also to Blass, Jebb, and Kenyon.

CONCORDANCE

These translations are principally based on the text of E. Diehl, *Anthologia Lyrica Graeca* (Vol. I [1936]; Vol. II [ed. of 1925]), except that the three selections from Bacchylides are based mainly on Edmonds, *Lyra Graeca*, and the one from Pindar follows Bowra's edition.

Since this is not a scholarly work, it may be sufficient to give the concordance of my selections with the numbers in Diehl.

LATTIMORE Archilochus	DIEHL
1	1
2	2
3	6
4	15
5	16
6	22
7	60
8	7
9	67
10	74
11	10
12	12
13	13
14	18
15	56
16	25
17	103
18	53
19	54
20	55
21	61
22	11
23	79
24	104
25	71
26	112
27	30

LATTIMORE Archilochus—*Continued*	DIEHL
28	94
29	88
30	58
31	62
32	64
33	66

Callinus

	DIEHL
1	1

Semonides

	DIEHL
1	7
2	1
3	3
4	6
5 ... Iamb. Ades.	1

Solon

	DIEHL
1	1
2	19
3	24

Tyrtaeus

	DIEHL
1	9
2	8

Hipponax

	DIEHL
1	24

GREEK LYRICS

Lattimore	Diehl	Lattimore	Diehl
Mimnermus		**Alcaeus**	
1...............	1	1...............	46
Alcman		2...............	78
1...............	1	3...............	90, 91
Sappho		4...............	94
1...............	1	**Anacreon**	
2...............	2	1...............	5
3...............	27	2...............	54
4...............	58		
5...............	59	**Simonides**	
6...............	98	1...............	13
7...............	158	2...............	48
Ibycus		3...............	6
1...............	6	4...............	7
		5...............	37
Stesichorus		6...............	4
1...............	17	7...............	42
2...............	11	8...............	20

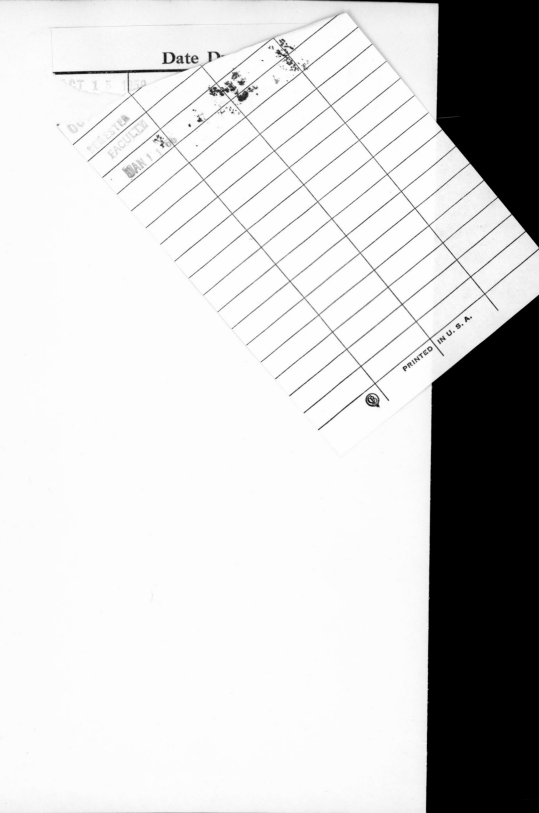